SEP 2 1 2007

WITHDRAWN
DOWNERS GROVE PUBLIC LIBRARY

 **W9-ATY-621**

Downers Grove Public Library
1050 Curtiss St.
Downers Grove, IL 60515

03/08 - 1

THE LITHOSPHERE

THE LITHOSPHERE

EARTH'S CRUST

GREGORY L. VOGT, Ed.D.

TWENTY-FIRST CENTURY BOOKS · MINNEAPOLIS

Twenty-First Century Books
A division of Lerner Publishing Group
241 First Avenue North
Minneapolis, Minnesota 55401 U.S.A.

Website address: www.lernerbooks.com

Library of Congress Cataloging-in-Publication Data

Vogt, Gregory.
    The lithosphere : Earth's crust / by Gregory L. Vogt.
       p.   cm. — (Earth's spheres)
    Includes bibliographical references and index.
    ISBN-13: 978–0–7613–2838–4 (lib. bdg. : alk. paper)
    ISBN-10: 0–7613–2838–6 (lib. bdg. : alk. paper)
    1. Earth—Crust—Juvenile literature. 2. Earth—Surface—Juvenile
literature. I. Title. II. Series: Vogt, Gregory. Earth's spheres.
QE511.V58 2007
551.1'36—dc22   2006014882

Manufactured in the United States of America
1 2 3 4 5 6 – DP – 12 11 10 09 08 07

CONTENTS

INTRODUCTION 6

BATTLEFIELD EARTH

CHAPTER 1 12

THE STUFF OF THE LITHOSPHERE

CHAPTER 2 28

JIGSAW PUZZLE

CHAPTER 3 41

BUILDING MOUNTAINS AND VALLEYS

CHAPTER 4 56

TEARING DOWN THE LAND

CONCLUSION 70

CHANGE AND BALANCE

GLOSSARY 74

BIBLIOGRAPHY 76

FOR FURTHER INFORMATION 77

INDEX 78

BATTLEFIELD
EARTH

For more than one hundred years, Earth has been under attack. First came invaders from space in science-fiction books. Later, movies and television awoke giant creatures from the depths of the oceans and from ruptured volcanic mountains. Humans have been toasted by Martian death rays and chased by bad-tempered lizards that stomped across cities. They have ducked fire-breathing dragons and battled with hunter robots and half human-half machine creatures.

These fictional assaults on Earth are great fun if you don't look at the science in them too carefully. But all of them fall short when it comes to what is really happening. There is a real battle going on for the surface of Earth that involves real forces more powerful than any dreamed of by science-fiction writers. It is a battle that has been raging for billions of years. In its wake are obliterated mountains, deep gorges, new islands, and folded and cracked rock thrusting upward above the ocean floors. The battle is between the forces of nature that shape the surface of Earth.

Sometimes the forces are very sudden and unimaginably violent such as the eruption of Mount Saint Helens, a volcano in Washington State, in May of 1980. In just seconds, the entire top and one side of the volcano blew away. Over the next several hours, the eruption rained 540 million tons (490 million metric tons) of pulverized rock across 22,000 square miles (57,000 sq. km) of land as far eastward

The Grand Canyon of the Colorado River is a dramatic example of the effects that water, wind, and weather can have on Earth's surface. The river has worked its way through layers of rock, creating a valley that is more than 1 mile (1.6 kilometers) deep in spots.

Just as water erodes some areas, it builds up others. This photo shows the delta formed by Africa's Nile River depositing sediment as it reaches the sea. The triangular Nile Delta is a highly fertile area about the size of the state of Massachusetts.

as Minnesota and Oklahoma. Other times, the destructive forces are terribly slow, such as the grinding force of the Colorado River. Nevertheless, over 10 million years, the Colorado carved the Grand Canyon, a gorge about 5,000 feet (1,500 meters) deep and up to 18 miles (29 km) wide!

Then, there are the constructive forces that slowly built up the Himalayas of Nepal to make them the highest mountains in the world. Rivers can construct as well as destruct. The Nile River has gradually deposited a triangular delta of sediment where it empties into the Mediterranean Sea. The Nile Delta area is a rich agricultural region where the topsoil can be as much as 70 feet (21 meters) deep. The Nile Delta is now the place where most Egyptians live.

The surface of planet Earth is an amazing place with huge oceans splotched with seven large continental landmasses and two ice caps and dotted with thousands of islands. The surface looks stable and secure, but that is because we look at it from the vantage of the human life span. In our fifty or one hundred years, we see little change other than the things we create such as cities and roads. But our best efforts are like chalk marks on a sidewalk. We may change the way the outermost few yards of the surface looks, but nature makes the really big changes over millions and billions of years.

LAND BUILDING, LAND WEARING

The forces of nature shaping Earth fall into two main categories. There are forces that build the land and forces that tear it down. The forces are in a dynamic balance. In some places, the building forces are winning, creating islands, broad plains, and long chains of mountains. In other places, balance occurs where the building and the tearing-down forces are equal. A broad plateau is uplifted while a great river slices a deep gorge through its surface. In still other places, the tearing-down forces take the lead and entire islands are worn down to the sea.

It is all very complex because Earth is a complex planet. Earth is far more than water and land. Earth is a

A cross section of Earth reveals sphere upon sphere. Beginning in the middle is an inner and outer core of metal only a few hundred miles (km) smaller in size that Earth's Moon. Surrounding the core is a thick mantle of very hot rock, and capping it is a cool thin crust of rock that makes up the hard outer shell of Earth. The lithosphere makes up the top portion of the mantle, just under the crust.

multilayered sphere. Seen from outer space, Earth is the third planet from the Sun. It is a rocky world 7,911 miles (12,740 km) in diameter. It has a large moon orbiting about it that is almost one-quarter of its diameter in size. Beneath its surface at its center, Earth has a great sphere, or core, of solid iron that is surrounded by molten iron. Surrounding the core is a rocky sphere, called the mantle. Near its surface, the rock is semisolid. It slowly flows with

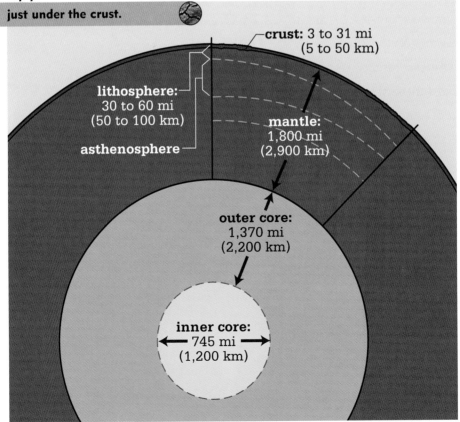

crust: 3 to 31 mi
(5 to 50 km)

lithosphere:
30 to 60 mi
(50 to 100 km)

asthenosphere

mantle:
1,800 mi
(2,900 km)

outer core:
1,370 mi
(2,200 km)

inner core:
745 mi
(1,200 km)

rising and falling heat currents, called convection cells. Resting above the mantle and including the mantle's uppermost layer is the lithosphere. It is an irregular rocky sphere at the surface that is thinner beneath the oceans and thicker where the continents are. Intermingled with the lithosphere are the hydrosphere—all of Earth's water; the biosphere—the zone where living things reside; and the atmosphere—a blanket of gas surrounding Earth. In its upper reaches, the atmosphere thins and becomes electrically charged as it meets the vacuum of outer space.

All of Earth's different spheres interact to mold and shape Earth's surface. This is the story of how one of Earth's spheres, the lithosphere, interacts with the other spheres to create the surface we live on. It is about the mountains and valleys, plains and plateaus, gorges and canyons, and the materials that make them up. It is about the forces that shape the surface and make a home for us to live on. Other books in this series will focus on the core and mantle, the hydrosphere, the atmosphere, the biosphere, and the outer atmosphere.

CHAPTER 1

The Stuff of the Lithosphere

The lithosphere is the outermost layer of Earth. Its surface is dimpled and pinched with deep ocean basins, where most of Earth's water collects, and puckered with lofty mountain peaks. The lithosphere part of the crust ranges from 30 to 60 miles (50 to 100 km) in thickness and consists of two parts. Most of the lithosphere is solid rock, but the rock gets softer, almost plastic in its lower levels where it overlaps with the upper mantle.

The upper part of the lithosphere is what we call the crust of Earth. The crust is divided into two distinct types, the ocean crust and the continental crust. The ocean crust is covered by the ocean. The continental crust is the part we live on. The

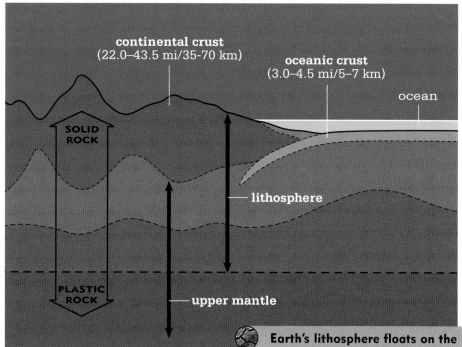

continental crust
(22.0–43.5 mi/35-70 km)

oceanic crust
(3.0–4.5 mi/5–7 km)

ocean

SOLID
ROCK

—lithosphere

PLASTIC
ROCK

—upper mantle

Earth's lithosphere floats on the mantle below. Lithosphere rock is solid at the surface but becomes hotter with depth and almost plastic so that it can slowly flow. The crust under the oceans is thin, but it is much thicker under the continents, especially beneath lofty mountains.

relatively thin ocean crust ranges from 3 to 4.5 miles (5 to 7 km) in depth, while the thicker continental crust ranges from 22 to 43.5 miles (35 to 70 km). That makes the continental crust about seven times thicker than the oceanic crust.

The lower part of the lithosphere overlaps part of the mantle beneath. This overlap zone is called the asthenosphere. The word means "weak." Asthenosphere rock is very hot and under great pressure from the crust above. The heat and pressure comes from the weight of the crust pressing down on it. The heat softens the rock, and the pressure causes it to flow very slowly.

13

The rocky crust actually floats on the asthenosphere. The crust is like a large piece of ice floating in water. Part of the ice rises above, and part is below the water. A thicker piece of ice presses deeper into the water and rises higher above it at the same time. Earth's crust is thickest under continents and mountains and thinnest under the oceans. The thicker continents press deeper into the asthenosphere than does the crust beneath the oceans.

Except for the upper few yards of the surface, which consists of a mishmash of rock, soil, liquid and frozen water, and living things, the bulk of lithosphere is rock. Rocks are the hard stuff of Earth we stand on. We see gravel rock in driveways, buildings faced with polished rock, boulders lying in fields, steep rocky cliffs and river-cut gorges, and snowcapped rocky mountains reaching thousands of feet (meters) above the plains.

Rocks are made up of minerals. Some rocks, such as granite, consist of interlocking grains of three or four minerals. Other rocks are made up of just one kind of mineral. Geologists, scientists who study the structure and materials of Earth, define minerals as natural materials made of atoms that are arranged in neat patterns to form a crystal structure. Crystals have many shapes, such as cubes, prisms, octahedrons (diamond shape), flat sheets, and needles. Minerals may have a shiny metal surface, be glassy, be dull and opaque, or be transparent. They come in all colors. Some, like diamonds, are very hard, and others, like talc, are very soft.

Minerals are very important to us because they provide the raw materials we use to make the things we depend upon. Automobiles, airplanes, computer chips, and windows are made from minerals, such as hematite (source of iron), bauxite (source of aluminum), and quartz (source of glass). Some minerals are in pure form, such as copper, which is used for electrical wire, and diamonds, which are used for cutting tools and jewelry. Other minerals are collections of many elements that have to be processed to extract the materials we need. Hematite is made of iron and oxygen. When hematite is processed, oxygen is removed and the iron is turned into steel.

One of the jobs of geologists is to find minerals that can be mined. To do that, they have to know a lot about rocks and how they are formed because it is in the rocks where the minerals are found. The mineral grains in many rocks are so small that you cannot see the crystal shapes except under a special microscope. Rarely, minerals like gold, silver, and copper fill in cracks in rocks to become veins that can easily be mined. Usually, rocks have to be crushed and treated with heat and chemicals to remove the needed minerals.

The most useful metals mined from Earth in order of their usefulness are iron, aluminum, copper, gold, nickel, platinum, tin, lead zinc, and molybdenum.

TELLING MINERALS APART

The rocks of Earth are made from combinations of about two thousand different minerals. Most minerals are very rare, and the bulk of Earth's crust is made from a handful of different kinds such as quartz, feldspar, mica, and calcite. Geologists look at the minerals in rocks to understand how the rocks were formed. They have to be able to recognize what the different minerals are.

Minerals have many properties that enable them to be identified. First is just how they look. They may have a metallic appearance like galena or glassy like olivine. They may be hard like topaz or soft like gypsum. They may have a crystal form that is easy to see like the paper-thin sheets of mica or the cube shape of pyrite. The color of the mineral is tricky because some minerals can come in many colors. Fluorite can be purple, blue, yellow, white, or green. However, if you drag a piece of fluorite across a rough ceramic tile, it will leave a white streak no matter what color it is. Then there are odd properties. If a geologist suspects a mineral is halite, the geologist will taste it to see if it is salty. Halite is the mineral form of salt. Some minerals are magnetic. Some minerals form cubic crystals, but when they break, they form diamond shapes.

Identifying minerals is like being a crime scene detective. Gather enough observations about the mystery mineral and eliminate all of the possible choices except one. Geologists then go one step further. For example, if a mineral in a rock usually forms as salty lakes dry up, the geologist has a pretty good idea of the history of that rock.

Minerals are the most common solid materials found on Earth. Although there are about two thousand different kinds of minerals, Earth's crust contains relatively few of them in abundance, among them *(from top)* quartz, feldspar, mica, and calcite. Each kind of mineral has a unique set of properties determined by its chemical composition and internal arrangement of atoms. In a quick glance, quartz and calcite could be mistaken for each other. They are quite different. Quartz is much harder than calcite, and calcite can be dissolved by acid. If you look closely at their crystal shapes, those are different too. Quartz breaks like glass, but calcite cleaves into rhombohedrons (like a cube that is skewed). Mica flakes in thin sheets, but feldspar breaks into chunks with some jagged sides and others smooth.

quartz

feldspar

mica

calcite

Basalt is an igneous rock, commonly found in the remains of old lava flows. The terraced appearance of this basalt hillside is due to the presence of several lava flows piled on top of one another.

Geologists have learned that rocks are created in three main ways. The building forces of Earth create some rocks while others are created by the destructive forces. The first way of creating rock involves Earth's tremendous interior heat. At various levels within Earth, rock is molten and is called magma. It slowly moves about within Earth, and when it nears the surface, it begins cooling. Large interlocking mineral crystals such as quartz, feldspar, and hornblende minerals may form, producing a rock type known as granite. Granite is often used for facing large office buildings, for countertops, and for tombstones.

Much later, the rock may be exposed at Earth's surface by the destructive forces of erosion. In many places around Earth, molten rock may follow cracks or melt its way to the surface. The magma, now called lava, hardens on the surface to form volcanic rock. Rocks that formed out of molten material below or above ground are called igneous rocks. *Igneous* means "fire-formed." Igneous rocks spewed out of volcanoes are also called volcanic rock. The term *lava* is used for both the molten material that spills on the surface and the rock that forms from it when it cools.

A second rock-forming process occurs when existing rocks are weathered, or changed, by the destructive forces of water, wind, and chemicals, and broken down into small boulders, pebbles, sand, or dust particles. Later, these particles accumulate into thick layers at the bottoms of oceans and lakes and become cemented together to form sedimentary rock.

This sedimentary rock was formed by layers of sediment carried in water or by air currents being compressed into rock. The thick horizontal lines were produced by changes in the direction of the currents over time.

ANIMAL ROCK BUILDERS

Thick layers of sedimentary limestone are found in many places around the world, including on the tops of mountains. Limestone layers were built by animals. Limestone is made of the mineral calcite (calcium carbonate). It is the stuff found in our bones, in coral, and in the shells of clams, snails, and tiny microscopic animals. When living, these animals float in the seawater or live on the shallow ocean bottoms. When the floaters die, their soft parts decompose, but the calcium carbonate in their hard parts settles on the bottom. They accumulate to form layers of calcareous ooze. In addition, ocean bottom-dwelling life adds thick layers of shells and coral skeletons to the ooze. Over eons of time, the layers turn into limestone. Often marks of the animals' shells and other structures are preserved in the rock as fossils.

Fossils show that certain forms of insects date back more than 350 million years. This dragonfly fossil, found in Brazil, dates from the early Cretaceous period, 145 million years ago.

Slate is a fine-grained metamorphic rock consisting mainly of grains of mica and quartz. Slate results when pressure in Earth's crust squeezes the mica and other minerals into parallel layers.

When mud hardens, it becomes the sedimentary rock called shale. Sometimes, chemical action of water dissolves away rock material entirely, and it later crystallizes in thick layers of minerals as the water evaporates. Limestone is formed from crystallized calcite or formed by creatures that have calcite skeletons. It is those skeletons that form coral reefs that later become limestone.

The third rock-forming process occurs when existing rock is subjected to lots of heat and pressure. This does not happen at the surface. It happens at depths of several miles beneath the surface. The pressure and heat changes the rock and makes it look very different from its parent rock. Rocks formed by this process are called metamorphic. Some of the conditions for making metamorphic rocks occur when tens of thousands of yards (meters) of sediment pile up in one location, pressing and heating the lowest layers, or the edges of large rock masses push against one another. When shale is exposed to metamorphism, it gets squeezed into a very thin and hard layer and becomes the rock slate. Slate was once used for school chalkboards because it is so hard and dense, and it is still used as a roofing material.

ROUND AND AROUND

Igneous, sedimentary, and metamorphic rocks each tell a story of Earth's formation. They are like a family photo album of Earth because these three rock types are the result of particular events that have taken place in Earth's past. However, unlike photos that freeze your appearance for all time, the three rock types in Earth's photo album continually change. Destructive forces can change an igneous rock into a sedimentary rock or a metamorphic rock into an igneous rock. Geologists call the path rock takes from one type to another the rock cycle.

To explain how the cycle works, let us start with molten magma and follow one particular rock type, granite. We have learned that granite is made from interlocking mineral crystals. For various reasons, which we will examine later, the rock (granite) formed from magma that cooled below the surface. Before it cooled, the magma was moving toward the surface making a

large blob in Earth.
This formed the basic
mountain. The blob
(batholith) cooled off
and became rock. Rain,
wind, ice, and gravity
gradually wear away
Earth above the granite,
eventually exposing the
granite and making the mountain
we see today. Quartz and other mineral
grains in the granite break away and become small
sand grains that are carried by rivers and deposited in
an ocean basin. Over long periods of time, chemicals in
the ocean water cement the grains together and
sandstone is formed. Sandstone is a sedimentary rock.
At some time later, so much rock piles up in the ocean
that the grains of quartz are heated and squeezed
together. The grains of quartz start gluing themselves
together with cement. Cementation forms the sediment
into a sedimentary rock. If the sedimentary rock is
smashed by a tectonic event (pieces of crust called
plates moving together), then the sedimentary rock
could be metamorphosed. This would turn the
sedimentary rock into a metamorphic rock. Finally, the
quartzite (this is a metamorphic rock) could be dragged
back down toward Earth's mantle where it is heated so
much that it melts to form magma again.

Igneous rocks
make up 95 percent of
the rocks in Earth's crust.
But 75 percent of the rocks on
Earth's surface are
sedimentary rocks and
metamorphic rocks.

HOW OLD?

Geologists say Earth formed 4.5 billion years ago. They say that the Appalachian Mountains were as big as the Rocky Mountains about 200 million years ago. They say that Crater Lake in Oregon was once a huge volcano, but 7,000 years ago, it exploded and collapsed, leaving a deep lake in the center of its cone. How do geologists know these things happened since none of them were around at the time? Geologists use a variety of techniques to estimate age.

One technique is relative age dating. If you pile pennies into a stack, you can say the bottom penny was the first penny to be placed on the stack and the top one was the last one to be placed on the stack. If geologists see a bunch of horizontal sedimentary rock layers, they are usually safe in saying the oldest rock is on the bottom and each layer above is younger than the one beneath it. If they find particular fossils in one rock layer and then a long distance away, they find another rock layer with the same kind of fossil, they can assume the rock is about the same age.

Relative age dating doesn't tell you how old anything is, but it does tell you which rock is older. Absolute age dating gives you numbers. There are many different ways to do this depending upon what is being dated. For example, geologists can drill a core out of the bottom of a lake and count layers of mud. Each layer represents sediment that was

As samples are pulled from the earth by a hollow drill, they are placed side-by-side in a core box and labeled with the depth from which the core sample was taken. Cores provide geologists with a profile of the kinds of rock beneath the surface.

deposited in a particular year. Counting the layers can indicate how old the lake is. The same can be done with the layers of ice in a glacier. The age of the Grand Canyon can be determined by estimating how rapidly the Colorado River cuts through the rock, but this does not tell us how old the rocks in the Grand Canyon are. It only tells us how long it took for the Grand Canyon to form. There is lots of guesswork in this because you have to know how the climate has changed during that time. Wetter periods mean more water and faster cutting. Nevertheless, the approximate age of the canyon can be determined by comparing the average erosion rate with the depth of the canyon.

Volcanic eruptions will create lots of ash that covers up forests. The age of the forest can be estimated by measuring the amount of carbon 14 present in the wood. Carbon 14 is one of many radioactive elements that give off particles and eventually change to another element. Geologists know how fast these elements change. By comparing the amount of the radioactive element with the element they have changed into, the geologists will get a good estimate of the age. When the age of the wood is determined, the date of the volcanic eruption can be determined.

Carbon 14 is good for dating the remains of living things to about 50,000 years ago. Older than that, there isn't enough carbon 14 left to make measurements. Other elements such uranium 238 and potassium 40 are good for measuring the age of rocks and minerals in the range of millions and billions of years because they decay much more slowly.

You might wonder why age dating is important. If you want to tell Earth's story, you need to know when things happened. Let's take a volcano as an example. There are lush forests and beautiful lakes on its sides. It looks like a beautiful place to build your home, but is it safe? If the history of the volcano shows that every 200 years or so there is a major eruption and the last one was 190 years ago, you might want to build somewhere else.

The rock cycle sounds like a very neat idea. Igneous rock turns to sedimentary rock, which turns to metamorphic rock, which turns to igneous rock again. It is not that simple. As we said earlier, Earth is very complex. Although rock generally changes from one type to another, it may take many side trips along the way. For example, the forces that create mountains may press on the igneous granite so much that it turns directly into the metamorphic rock gneiss without becoming a sedimentary rock first. (Gneiss is pronounced "nice," which leads to many bad geologist jokes. "Oh, look. Isn't that a gneiss rock?")

Before layers of sedimentary sandstone can be changed into metamorphic or igneous rock, they may be cut into again by rivers, breaking loose the grains of sand. Each time this happens, the grains are worn smaller as they make their way downriver and pile up in sandbars. Eventually, the sandbars get cemented together to form new sandstone. However, before the sediment can become rock, it may again be moved by rivers several times before it is finally deposited where it will become rock. Millions of tons of sediment is washed down the rivers of the world every year and deposited in oceans where it will eventually harden into rocks.

Metamorphic rocks too may be eroded to form sedimentary rock. Finally, igneous rock may never reach the surface. Conditions underground may change, causing granite to melt back into magma, which later spurts up to the surface as lava.

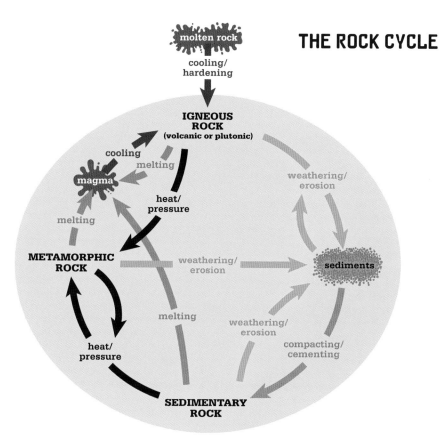

THE ROCK CYCLE

The rock cycle is a way of showing the relationships of Earth's different rocks and the processes that created them. Starting with molten rock, the first solid rock type is igneous rock. There are many paths that can be taken. The arrows show different routes. For example, sedimentary rock could be subjected to weathering and erosion and become sediment again. Or sedimentary rock could be heated and pressed to become metamorphic rocks. Geologists look for clues in the structure and minerals of rock to tell their story.

You can see the complexities of the rock cycle by laying it all out in a diagram. The main cycle goes around the outside, and all the side trips are shown with curved arrows crossing the middle. The rock cycle enables geologists to trace the history of a rock or mineral back millions or billions of years.

27

CHAPTER 2

Jigsaw Puzzle

German meteorologist Alfred Wegener (1880–1930) was not the first to observe how the continents fit together like a puzzle, but he was the first to offer proof. Like the mapmakers of the sixteenth century, Wegener noticed the odd shape of the world's continents. If you could push North and South America eastward and Europe and Africa westward, the continents would almost fit together. Furthermore, the continent of Australia looks as though it would fit next to India, and the island nation of Madagascar would certainly fit in a notch on the eastern side of Africa. The fit gets even better if the edge of the continental shelf is used for the borders of the pieces. The continental shelf is the gentle slope of the continents as they

descend beneath the water to an average depth of 430 feet (130 m). After that, the continents dip more steeply and transition from continental crust into oceanic crust. The implication of this observation is that the continents were once joined together in a supercontinent and something caused it to break apart and for the pieces to move away from one another.

Unlike the mapmakers, Wegener offered more than just the observation that the continents looked like they were once together. Wegener offered proof in a paper he published in 1912. He noted that the kinds of rocks on both sides of the Atlantic matched up like the pictures on a jigsaw puzzle. When you assemble a picture puzzle, you look not only at the shapes of the interlocking pieces but also at what is pictured on each piece. Even though two pieces might fit together, if one shows a flower and the other a dog, the pieces really don't fit. Wegener showed that the pieces of the continents did seem to fit because the rock types on both sides matched. Other proof included finding similar fossils on both sides. Fossils are the remains or imprints of ancient life that have been preserved in stone. Furthermore, scratch marks of ancient glaciers are aimed in similar directions on opposite sides as well.

Although not necessarily against Wegener's hypothesis that the continents have drifted apart, critics pointed out that for his hypothesis to be true, there had to be some way for the continents to move. They couldn't just plow their way across the ocean

This computerized image of the globe shows the supercontinent Pangea. It is believed to have formed about 300 million years ago, when most of Earth's land surface moved together due to continental drift. About 100 million years later, the landmass broke up again. This led to the formation of the continents.

floor as Wegener seemed to indicate. There had to be some mechanism for this to take place, but no one had an answer. Several decades later, the U.S. Navy came to the rescue.

During World War II (1939–1945), Harry Hess (1902–1969), a geology teacher turned naval officer, came up with a program to locate enemy submarines. He tested his ideas on board a ship that sailed the North Atlantic. After proving the idea worked, he served in the Pacific Ocean and used sounding equipment to map the ocean's floor. Sounding equipment emits sound waves that strike the ocean floor and bounce back to microphones on the ship. The time it took for the sound to bounce back told Hess how deep the ocean floor was at that location. Gradually, while crisscrossing the Pacific, Hess was able to make maps that covered large portions of the ocean floor. After the war, the navy continued mapping the ocean floor.

In time, the floors of all the world's oceans were mapped. An astounding discovery was made that helped Hess answer the question of how the continents move. The world's longest mountain chain lies beneath the oceans. It is 50,000 miles (80,000 km) long and circles Earth in a twisting path. Under the North and South Atlantic Oceans, the chain snakes midway between the continents in the North and South Atlantic. Its course is roughly the same shape as the edges of the continents to either side. Furthermore, mapping the ocean floors revealed a rift, or deep valley, that runs the length of the mountain chain. Called the Great Global Rift,

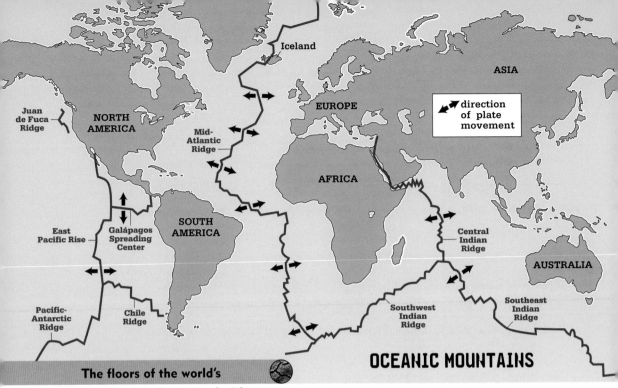

Iceland

ASIA

EUROPE

direction of plate movement

Juan de Fuca Ridge

NORTH AMERICA

Mid-Atlantic Ridge

AFRICA

East Pacific Rise

Galápagos Spreading Center

SOUTH AMERICA

Central Indian Ridge

AUSTRALIA

Pacific-Antarctic Ridge

Chile Ridge

Southwest Indian Ridge

Southeast Indian Ridge

OCEANIC MOUNTAINS

The floors of the world's oceans are crisscrossed with a long chain of mountains. The mountains mark where new crust is forming from molten material pushed up through cracks. The cracks are being spread by the pressure of new material from below.

the valley is actually a crack that appears to be getting wider.

Harry Hess proposed a startling idea that was later refined by many geologists into a worldwide theory of plate tectonics. The modern version of this theory is that the world's crust is broken into seven large plates and several smaller plates that move very slowly, about 1 inch (2.5 centimeters) a year. In some areas, the plates spread apart. In other areas, the plates collide. In still other areas, the plates slide past one another. Some of the plates carry the world's continents on their backs, while others form the bottoms of the oceans. As we will see later, plate tectonics helps geologists explain the presence of many of the world's mountains and earthquakes.

Other geologists got into the act and began dredging up rock samples from the rift, the mountain chains, and from the ocean floor on either side. The ages of the rocks provided another important clue. Rocks from the Great Global Rift are the youngest. On either side of the mountains, the rocks get older the farther away you get from them.

For a long time, geologists wondered why the accumulation of sediment, mud, and silt on the ocean floor was relatively thin, even though the oceans had been around for billions of years. What was happening to the sediments? Furthermore, fossils of sea life dredged up from the ocean bottom were relatively young—no older than 180 million years. Plate tectonics was the answer.

This fissure in Thingvellir, Iceland, is part of the Mid-Atlantic Ridge. In the north, the ridge forms the boundary between the North American and Eurasian tectonic plates. These plates are moving apart along the ridge allowing magma from beneath Earth's crust to well up. Iceland is entirely volcanic in origin and is one of the few places where the Mid-Atlantic Ridge can be seen above sea level.

Along the Mid-Atlantic Ocean Ridge, new igneous rock is continually forming. The rock is pushing up from Earth's mantle below. As the new rock pushes upward, existing rock is shoved to either side. At the same time, the new rock creates the undersea mountain chain and the rift running along its middle (mid-oceanic ridge).

The creation of new rock means that in other places, rock has to be returned to the mantle or else Earth's surface would be nothing more than a huge pileup of mountains. Where does the old rock go?

All of North and South America and the western half of the floor of the North and South Atlantic Oceans are riding on huge plates. These plates are being pushed west and northwest by the new rock forming at the Mid-Atlantic Ridge. As these plates move west, they collide with the Pacific Plate (Pacific Ocean bottom) and some smaller plates running along the western side of South America. The collision is like a very slow traffic accident between a tractor trailer and a small sports car. When these vehicles collide head-on, the tractor trailer is only affected a little, while the sports car gets smashed and shoved under the truck. The collision of the plates produces large mountains on the western edges of North and South America. Both continents have long chains of mountains along their western coastlines. This is called a subduction zone.

Folded marine sedimentary rocks and bits of ancient ocean floor are strong evidence that the Appalachian Mountains were formed more than 480 million years ago

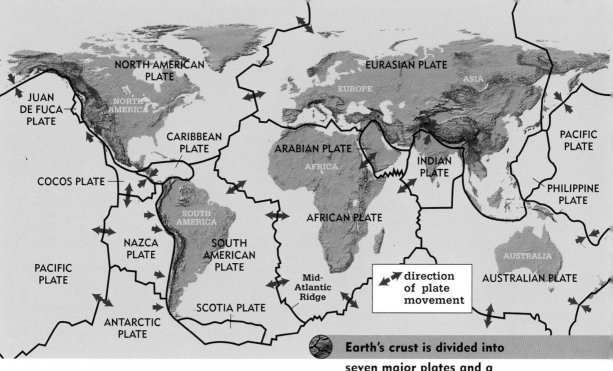

Earth's crust is divided into seven major plates and a number of smaller plates that are slowly moving across Earth's surface. Where plates collide, new mountains are pushed up, volcanoes form, and many earthquakes occur.

by the collision of two continental plates. These are huge slow-moving collisions that produce many earthquakes but few volcanoes.

On the eastern side of the Atlantic, the African and the Eurasian plates are being driven northeastward by the pressure of the new rock forming in the mid-oceanic ridge. These plates ultimately collide with the western edge of the Pacific Plate, creating a lengthy chain of mountains there that connect with the northern end of the American coastal mountains. These are not the only mountains produced by the moving plates. The plate carrying India is shoving into the Eurasian plate. The collision there has produced the world's highest mountains, the Himalayas.

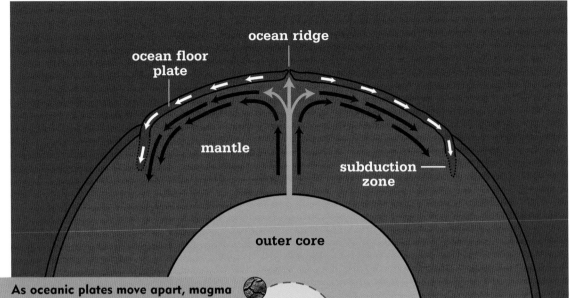

ocean ridge

ocean floor
plate

mantle

subduction —
zone

outer core

As oceanic plates move apart, magma
rises through the gap, cooling to form
mountain chains along ocean ridges.
The ocean plates move away from the
ridge and toward the continental
plates. When these plates collide, the
ocean plate is driven downward into
the mantle (subduction zone), where
the rock is recycled.

As in a car accident, where the
front end of one car may ride up and
over and the front end of the other car
is pushed down and under, the
collision of plates produces upward
and downward movements. Ocean
plates are thinner and denser than continental plates. When
an ocean plate collides with a continental plate, the ocean
plate is driven downward. As the ocean plate material
moves downward, it is heated and melts. Some of the ocean
crust is eventually absorbed back into the mantle. The rest
forms big batholiths of magma that rise toward the surface.
Near the surface the magma may cool and form granite, or
it may break through the surface in a volcanic eruption.

This is the answer to what ultimately happens to all
the rock formed in the Great Global Rift. It also answers
the question of why ocean sediments are not thicker.

PACIFIC RING OF FIRE

When geologists began plotting the locations of the world's earthquakes, a startling pattern appeared. A large number of earthquakes occur at or very near the edge of the continents and the islands that ring the Pacific Ocean. The pattern became more startling when the world's active volcanoes were plotted on the map too. Most of them followed the ring too. The pattern was nicknamed the Ring of Fire. The majority of the world's earthquakes and volcanoes follow the margins of the tectonic plates of Earth. The most intense activity occurs where plates collide and ocean crust is driven down to the mantle. The melting that occurs along the way releases molten magma that works its way back to the surface along cracks produced by an earthquake or by melting the "country rock." Seafloor spreading in the Great Global Rift also accounts for many earthquakes.

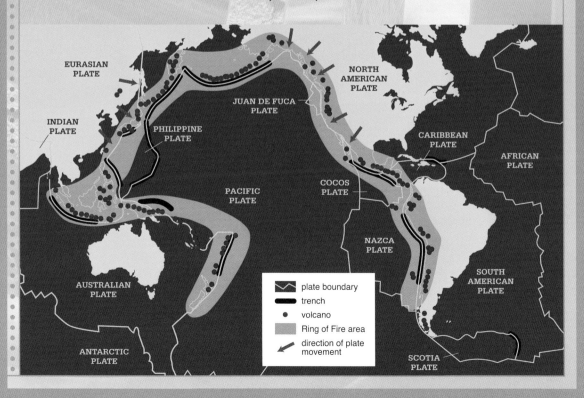

EURASIAN PLATE

INDIAN PLATE

PHILIPPINE PLATE

JUAN DE FUCA PLATE

NORTH AMERICAN PLATE

CARIBBEAN PLATE

AFRICAN PLATE

PACIFIC PLATE

COCOS PLATE

NAZCA PLATE

SOUTH AMERICAN PLATE

AUSTRALIAN PLATE

ANTARCTIC PLATE

SCOTIA PLATE

plate boundary
trench
volcano
Ring of Fire area
direction of plate movement

Ocean plates carry the sediment with them as they dive back to the mantle.

THE DRIVING FORCE

One big question needs to be answered to accept the theory of continental drift. What causes the new rock to form in the Great Global Rift? To answer that, we need to look to Earth's interior. Earth's mantle extends from the liquid core to the lower zone of the lithosphere. It is a shell about 1,800 miles (2,900 km) thick.

The temperature of the mantle ranges from 1,832°F (1,000°C) near the lithosphere to about 7,200°F (4,000°C) near the core. This is hot enough to melt any rock. This makes the upper mantle soft and semisolid. However, the rock near the bottom of the mantle is hard because of the weight of all the material above it.

Where does the heat come from? Some of it comes just from the weight of the material pressing on it. Miners descending in deep mines know that Earth's temperature increases about 45°F (25°C) with every 0.6 miles (1 km) of depth. The heat produced by pressure is insignificant compared to the two major sources of heat in Earth's interior. One major source of heat came with the formation of Earth more than 4 billion years ago. Earth and the whole solar system formed from a great cloud of gas and dust called a nebula. When gravity caused the cloud to contract, dust, elements, and gas collected in clumps that became the Sun and planets. Tremendous amounts of pressure and heat were generated as matter fell upon matter. Earth took shape as a large sphere of molten rock and metal. About half the heat in the mantle and core is actually left over from Earth's formation. Heat is a by-product of radioactive decay, so the remainder of the heat comes from the decay of radioactive elements such as uranium and thorium.

Imagine a boiling pot of water before the spaghetti is dropped in. The water heats up at the bottom of the kettle and rises to the surface. Cooler water at the surface falls to the bottom to be heated. Then it rises. The circular path of rising and falling water in the kettle is called a convection current. A similar thing happens in the mantle. Huge convection currents mix the semisolid mantle rock. The rate of mixing is very slow, and the rock flows only a few inches per year. In some places, such as beneath the Great Global Rift, the currents rise upward, create new igneous rock, and drive the crustal plates to the sides. In other places, the currents descend deeply into the mantle. They carry surface rock brought down by the collision of continental and ocean plates. This, in turn, helps the Great Global Rift to spread. To visualize what happens, slide a tablecloth off the end of a smooth table. When enough of the tablecloth is hanging off the end, it will pull the rest of the tablecloth along with it as it falls to the floor. The tablecloth is like the ocean crust that is being dragged downward to the

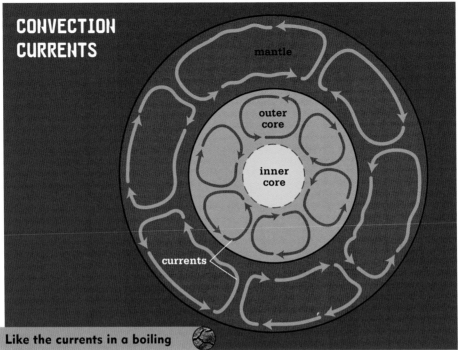

CONVECTION CURRENTS

mantle

outer core

inner core

currents

Like the currents in a boiling pot of water, convection currents occur within the soft superheated rock of the core and the mantle. Upwelling currents in the mantle drive molten material to the surface to form new crust. Downward currents return old crust to the mantle for recycling.

mantle in the collision zones with the thicker continental crust.

The result of the movement of the crustal plates over millions and billions of years is a complete reworking of the ocean crust. Continental plates split apart, drift away, collide with ocean plates, crumple the crust to form mountains, and recycle ancient surface rock. This has led to a wonderfully diverse surface on Earth's continents and islands. But it is not the whole story of how they were shaped.

CHAPTER 3

Building Mountains and Valleys

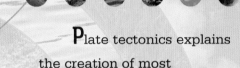

Plate tectonics explains
the creation of most
mountains on Earth's lithosphere.
But there is much more to building
mountains and volcanoes in subduction zones. For
example, the Hawaiian Islands are in the middle of the
Pacific Plate. Mauna Loa and Mauna Kea are 13,700-foot-
high (4,200 m) mountains that make up the big island
Hawaii. How were these mountains formed? Other
mountains and valleys are the result of earthquake
movements. What happens when rock breaks?

HOT SPOTS

There is an interesting observation about the
Hawaiian Islands. The islands are all different

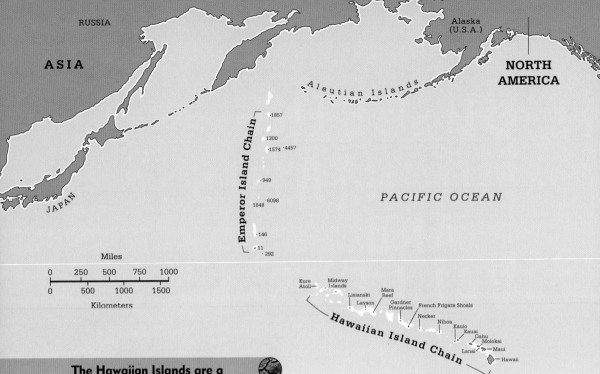

RUSSIA

Alaska
(U.S.A.)

ASIA

NORTH
AMERICA

Aleutian Islands

Emperor Island Chain

·1857

1300

·1574 ·4457

·949

·6098

1848

·146

·11

· 292

PACIFIC OCEAN

Miles

| 0 | 250 | 500 | 750 | 1000 |

| 0 | 500 | 1000 | 1500 |

Kilometers

Kure
Atoll

Midway
Islands

Lisianski

Layson

Mara
Reef

Gardner
Pinnacles

French Frigate Shoals

Necker

Nihoa

Kaulo

Kauai

Oahu

Molokai

Lanai

Maui

Hawaii

Hawaiian Island Chain

**The Hawaiian Islands are a
small part of the Hawaiian-
Emperor Island Chain, an
immense, mostly underwater
mountain chain of more than
80 volcanoes.**

ages. To the west is Kauai. It is 5 million years old. Oahu, 300 miles (500 km) to the east, is about 3 million years old. The largest island of the chain is Hawaii, and it is the youngest. Hawaii is 220 miles (350 km) east of Oahu, and it is still growing. The Hawaiian Islands form more or less a straight line, and if you extend the line to the west, you will come across more islands that get older and older the farther west you go. Eventually, you reach Midway Island, which is 1,600 miles (2,600 km) from Kauai and 28 million years old. The line continues on but bends to the north. You pass the 43-million-year-old Yuryaku, and then you reach the 65-million-year-old Suiko Seamount near the Alaskan Aleutian Islands.

RICH SOIL FROM VOLCANOES

There is a bright side to volcanoes. Volcanoes create new land. The islands of Hawaii were created by huge mounds of lava spewing through cracks in the Pacific Ocean floor. When the lava rocks finally extended above the ocean surface, the destructive forces of weathering and erosion attacked the lava. The new material brought by them to the surface is immediately attacked by the destructive forces of weathering and erosion. Volcanic rock and ash forms the basis for very rich soil. Many of the volcanic islands in tropical climates are among the most beautiful places in the world, with gently sloping mountain peaks, high waterfalls, and lush valleys. Flowers grow in abundance, and the soils are perfect for growing coffee, fruits, and vegetables.

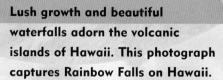

 Lush growth and beautiful waterfalls adorn the volcanic islands of Hawaii. This photograph captures Rainbow Falls on Hawaii.

All of these islands link up to make the Hawaiian-Emperor Island Chain. At one time, each of these islands was centered over a stable hot spot in the Pacific Ocean about where Hawaii is today. Hot spots occur in a number of places around the world. Yellowstone National Park is another of these locations, and the heat there creates a wonderland of geysers, hot springs, and fumaroles (a hole in the ground from which steam escapes). The world's largest hot spot is probably the one under Hawaii.

Hot spots are places where great convection currents rise within Earth's mantle. Although not permanent fixtures within the mantle, these spots last for tens of millions of years (60 million years for the Emperor-Hawaiian Chain). There isn't any splitting of the crust over a hot spot as there is over the convection currents that form the Great Global Rift. Instead, the heat rises to the surface in the form of molten lava through pipelike cracks. At the surface, the lava piles up and cools to form volcanic mountains or it spreads out and cools in large, more or less thick sheets of lava called flood basalts. In both cases, new land is created by the hot spots.

The existance of the Hawaiian-Emperor Island Chain is an important proof of the theory of plate tectonics. It shows that the Pacific Plate is moving to the west and north. The Suiko Seamount was one of the first volcanoes to form over the hot spot. Lava piled up to form the island, but gradually the Pacific Plate carried the island away from the hot spot.

The volcanic eruptions on the island stopped. Lava from the hot spot found a new way to the surface, and a new island was formed. It too was carried away by the moving plate and so on. In 65 million years, the Pacific Plate has moved 3,400 miles (5,500 km) to the west and north. Today even the big island of Hawaii is being moved off the hot spot and a new volcanic island in the chain is forming. The volcano is called Loihi, but you can't see it unless you have a submarine. The volcano has risen 3,054 feet (931 m) off the ocean floor. It still has 3,179 feet (969 m) to go before it pops above the surface of the Pacific Ocean and becomes an island. That should happen anytime between the next ten thousand and one hundred thousand years.

VOLCANIC MOUNTAINS

Volcanoes are the primary source of new rock created on the surface of the crust. Volcanoes take on many forms depending upon their location and the kind of lava that makes them up. The Hawaiian Island volcanoes form over stable hot spots in the mantle. From the side view, the two volcanoes Mauna Loa and Mauna Kea have very gradual slopes. These are called shield volcanoes. Volcanic mountains formed near the collision zones of continental and oceanic plates tend to have very steep sides. Mount Rainier in Washington State and Mount Fuji in Japan are good examples of these kinds of volcanoes. These are called composite volcanoes.

COMPLEX PLUMBING

Yellowstone National Park is just one of many places where you can find geysers, and many of the world's most impressive geysers are located there. Geysers can occur where there are hot spots in the upper mantle. One such spot is beneath Yellowstone. It is an unstable area that has had many earthquakes in the past. The rock beneath the park is fractured and cracked. Rainwater and meltwater from winter snows seep down the cracks and reach depths where the temperature is well above the boiling point. Pressures are great enough there to keep the water from boiling, but convection currents in the water carry the heat up to the surface where the pressure drops. Steam forms instantly and shoots to the surface. If the path is clear, the steam

Old Faithful erupts in Wyoming's Yellowstone National Park. The geysers and thermal springs in Yellowstone are evidence of a huge amount of underground activity from about 160,000 years ago. At that time, the area was the center of a massive volcanic eruption.

Water in the Morning Glory Pool of the Upper Geyser Basin in Yellowstone National Park glows under a cloudless, blue sky. Specialized bacteria that can live in this harsh environment have turned the edges of the pool yellow and orange. The hot spots below Yellowstone have created many thermal pools such as this one.

comes out as a cloud of vapor like steam from a teakettle. The hole the steam comes out of is called a fumarole. Sometimes, this vent is filled with water and the steam just bubbles through it. This is a hot spring. Geysers occur when the cracks beneath the ground have water-filled pockets. Steam starts collecting in the pockets. Eventually, so much steam collects that it spills out into the main cracks that reach the surface. Much like shaking a warm can of soda and then popping the lid, the steam blows out the water collected in the cracks. At the surface vent, water and steam rocket skyward.

A shield volcano forms when lava erupts from several different places. It then spreads out to build up a low, broad mountain. Most shield volcanoes have a number of craters on their summits. An aerial photograph shows this view of a crater at the summit of Hawaii's Mauna Loa, the world's largest volcano. The dark stripes on the slopes are lava flows.

Why do hot-spot volcanoes have gentle slopes and volcanoes in plate collision zones have steep slopes? A lot of it has to do with the lava that makes them up. Hawaiian Island lava tends to flow like thick syrup. Mount Rainier and Mount Fuji lava is stiff. As magma approaches Earth's surface, it contains lots of dissolved gas similar to gas in soft drinks. If the magma is runny, the gas can easily escape. During a Hawaiian volcano eruption, the dissolved gas (steam and other gases) rapidly expands because the pressure near the volcano's vent is much less than it was deep below the volcano. The gas blasts upward and creates lava fountains that shoot red-hot lava hundreds of yards (meters) into the air. The lava falls to the ground around the vent and cools and hardens and forms a small cone that gets taller and taller as more lava pours down on its sides. A lava lake starts forming in the mouth of the cone as more and more lava reaches the surface. Occasionally, a part of the hardened cone breaks like a dam and the lava in the lake flows through the gap and down the flank of the volcano. If the land is steep, the lava reaches speeds of 6 miles (10 km) per hour. Eventually, the lava cools and hardens. The overall effect is to widen the base of the volcano. In a later eruption, a new lava lake may escape along a different side of the cone and widen the volcano's base in that direction. Because the lava is runny, the lava spreads great distances to make a very wide base. Over a million years, a giant volcano such as Mauna Loa is created. Hawaiian Island volcano eruptions are relatively quiet, and except when a lava flow is coming, people can live in relative safety on the volcano's flanks. Even though Mauna Loa is the world's most active volcano, there is a national park and a hotel halfway up its summit and even an eighteen-hole golf course.

Mount Rainier grows in a similar way, but the sticky lava builds up a steep-walled cone. The cone builds upward. The hardened lava in the volcano's cone becomes a giant plug that stops up the volcano. Slowly, hot lava presses on the base of the plug. Pressure builds until the weight of the plug can no longer hold it. The pressure causes thousands of small earthquakes that fracture the cone. Finally, an explosion occurs that pulverizes lava rock and sends an ash plume tens of thousands of yards (meters) into the air. Any person or any animal near the volcano during the eruption will most likely be killed, and large expanses of forests will be incinerated. If one of these volcanoes has lots of snow and ice at its summit, the eruption will cause even more damage. During the

Mount Rainier, a peak in the state of Washington, is an example of a composite volcano. Its tall, steep sides have been built up over time as lava flowed out of one crater.

eruption, the ice will melt and mix with volcanic ash. Tremendous steaming flash floods roar down the mountain, carrying away anything in their path.

Mount Rainier in Washington State is considered one of North America's most dangerous volcanoes. Many people live near its flanks and could be killed if it explosively erupts as the nearby Mount Saint Helens did in 1980.

FOLDED MOUNTAINS

Folded mountains are formed by colliding continental plates. Look at a map of the eastern United States. You will see a series of mountain ridges that run parallel to the Atlantic coastline. These mountains are the Appalachians and consist of parallel ridges and valleys running between them. It is a part of a very large mountain chain that extends from Canada to Alabama and as far westward as Arkansas and Oklahoma. If you could take a giant knife and cut an east-west slice across Pennsylvania or across West Virginia, you would see a curious series of bends. It would look like the edge of a blanket bunched at the end of a bed. Layers of sedimentary and metamorphic rocks are bent to make the ridges and valleys. The folds that bend over like domes are called anticlines. The folds that bend downward like basins are called synclines.

Limestone layers in Dorset, England, are steeply folded, showing both anticlines and synclines.

The squeezing pressure that very gradually bent the rocks came from the collision of the American and the African plates. Over many millions of years, mountains were bent upward that would rival any mountain chain in the world today. However, the main episode that pushed up these mountains ended 225 million years ago. Erosion has since worn away thousands of feet (meters) of rocks from the mountaintops and deposited the sediment in the valleys. These mountains are thought to be the remnants of mountains that were as tall as the Himalayas.

CRACKING THE LAND

While the northeastern part of the Appalachians was folding, the mountains along the southern end of the chain were forming primarily through large fractures called faults. A fault is a crack that runs across rock. Usually, the rock shifts along the fault. One side goes up and the other goes down, or the rocks on opposite sides of the fault shift horizontally to one another. Earthquakes occur when the rocks on one or both sides suddenly shift. The greater the shift, the more violent the earthquake. Many faults move so slowly that they are hardly noticeable, but over millions of years, they can still push up giant mountains. The Himalayan mountains are the result of long-term faulting and continent-to-continent collision.

Faulting of the crust is caused by pressure or tension. As crustal plates move against one another, pushing and pulling forces are exerted on the rock. Most of the action occurs in the broad zones where the plates are in contact. But very large movements can occur in mid-continental regions. Some of the greatest North American earthquakes that ever took place were three that struck near New Madrid, Missouri, in 1811 and 1812. The quakes shook and jumbled the land, created new lakes, and caused shaking of some of the land that went on continually for weeks.

When the fault is caused by inward pressure, the rock on one side of the fault will usually ride up and over the other. Sometimes, the other side will drop down as well. If the pressure is aimed in opposite directions like automobile traffic on both sides of a highway, one or both sides will move horizontally.

FINDING EARTHQUAKES

You don't have to be anywhere near an earthquake to know where it happened. Many earthquakes occur in inaccessible locations such as along the submerged Mid-Atlantic Ridge. Earthquakes are easily found with devices called seismographs that record the strength and duration of the waves or vibrations created by earthquakes. When an earthquake occurs, vibrations travel across Earth's surface and through its interior. The way the vibrations pass through Earth have given scientists important clues that enabled them to discover its inner structure. The vibrations can also tell us when and where an earthquake occurred.

If you have at least three seismographs recording the same earthquake, the data they collect can be compared to give you the quake's location. If the waves reach one seismograph before they reach the others, it means the focus of the quake is nearest that station. The arrival times of the waves at each of the seismographs will be compared and the distance to the focus will be determined. For example, if the quake is 600 miles (966 km) from the first seismograph, a circle with a radius of 600 miles (966 km) will be drawn on a map around the location of that seismograph. The quake will be somewhere on the line of that circle. When the earthquake waves reach the second seismograph, a circle will be drawn around it to represent its distance from the quake. The two circles will cross each other in two places. The quake will either be at one intersection point or the other. When the circle for the third seismograph is drawn, this circle will intersect with the other two circles at only one place. Thus, the location of the earthquake has been found.

The famous San Andreas Fault in California that is responsible for a terrible earthquake in San Francisco in 1906 is a fault like this. The piece of crust that holds most of the California coastline is moving northward along the fault line. In a few million years, Los Angeles could move far enough to become a suburb of San Francisco.

Finally, if rock is pulling away from the fault line, one side will drop down in relation to the other. This has the effect of stretching the land. The upside of the fault may become a mountain while the downside becomes a valley.

One of the world's great seismic faults, the San Andreas extends almost the full length of California. The fault marks the boundary between the Pacific and North American tectonic plates. The fault is a source of earthquakes because these plates are moving past each other horizontally.

TEARING DOWN THE LAND

If the forces building mountains were the only forces at work, all of Earth's surface would be covered with several giant mountain ranges.

Fortunately, as soon as any bit of land appears above the oceans, destructive forces begin attacking it. These forces are responsible for the shape of nearly all the land we live on. They create great and small valleys and plains that are covered with grasslands, forests, and marshes. The constructive, or land-building, forces provide Earth's surface with its raw material, and the destructive, or land-tearing-down, forces shape the raw material into sediment such as sand and soil. All the plants and animals of the biosphere that live on Earth's continents depend upon the balancing of the two forces.

Massive exploding volcanoes and asteroids (giant space rocks ten to hundreds of feet/meters in size) or comets (giant space ice balls) occasionally collide with Earth and blast out large craters. Yet most destructive forces are very slow and quiet. But, like the race in the tortoise and the hare fable, slow-acting forces can accomplish great things if enough time is available.

Two major destructive forces act on Earth's land. One is called weathering and the other erosion. Weathering sounds like weather, and weather is certainly a big part of it but not all. You have seen houses in need of paint. What happened to the old paint? Sunlight, rain, and wind have weathered, or worn away the old paint. Sunlight, rain, and wind plus a number of other forces can wear away rock. Rock can be cooked by the heat of the day, causing it to expand slightly. At night the rock is chilled and it contracts slightly. In our lifetime, the effect is hardly noticeable, but it gradually takes its toll. Very tiny cracks may form. Water can get into the cracks. Winter freezing causes ice to form, pushing on the cracks and widening them. Plant roots will work their way into the cracks and grow and expand the cracks further. Eventually, the rock breaks.

Cracking in the rock can also be initiated by the Moon's gravitational pull on Earth. The Moon affects Earth's hydrosphere by creating ocean tides. To a lesser extent, the Moon also produces a tide in the solid crust of Earth. The crust is believed to rise and fall about 1 foot

The alternate freezing (expansion) and thawing (contraction) of water in cracks can eventually break a large boulder into pieces.

(30 cm) because of this attraction. In time, the rock is broken into pebbles and then sand and then soil. The general term for this debris is sediment. Much of Earth's solid surface is covered with sediment of one form or another created from rock. Although sediment piles up, the piles are temporary because of erosion. Erosion carries the sediment to low spots on Earth such as deep valleys and ocean bottoms. If the sediment remains there long enough, it turns into new rock that will someday be lifted above the surface to be worn and eroded again.

The most effective form of erosion is running water in rivers. Rivers start out as trickling streams on high ground where there is more rain or snow meltwater than can sink into the ground. They grow as streams merge and flow together. Eventually, the streams collect enough water that they become rivers that can cross continents.

The great and small rivers of the world carry sediment from high places and distribute it to low places. Although water is a liquid, it exerts tremendous force when it flows. If you have ever tried to walk across a fast-moving stream, you know this. It is easy to get swept away. Running water picks up and carries the finest mineral grains and pushes along pebbles and boulders. As the water passes over rock layers, the grains and pebbles and boulders grind against the surface of the rock. Fragments are ground off and carried with the rest of the sediment. The rock surface becomes gouged and sharp edges are smoothed. It is quite like sanding a piece of wood. In this way, the stream or river cuts downward through the rock.

How fast a stream cuts through rock is determined by how tough the rock is (softer rock grinds faster) and by the speed of the water. Streams in mountainous areas flow down steep slopes. The water travels very rapidly and is quite forceful. Pushing along everything from sand to boulders, the water grinds and cuts through the rock very quickly and leaves a relatively straight V-shaped valley.

Downstream, the slope of the land becomes more gradual. Different streams begin joining so that there is much more water flowing, but the speed of the water drops off. The large boulders and pebbles travel much more slowly, and only the finer particles continue to flow with the water. The grinding action is greatly reduced. The rate of erosion diminishes, and the river channel

Once a river is mature, the running water will slow, and the river will begin to meander—cutting a curved, looping path along the valley floor. This picture shows the San Juan River in Utah.

wanders, or snakes about, the valley floor. The valley takes on a U shape.

Still farther downstream, where the river approaches the ocean, water speed drops even further. Only silt is carried by the river, giving it a muddy appearance. The river breaks into many small channels that diverge and rejoin repeatedly to give a braided look. Occasionally a wide bend in the river closes off when sediment is deposited at its upper and lower ends. This creates a crescent-shaped lake called an oxbow lake. In time, the river water empties into the ocean. All the remaining sediment falls to the bottom. The sediment piles up to form a triangular-shaped marshy and muddy plain called a delta.

ALL RIVERS FLOW TO THE SOUTH—NOT!

When you look at a map of the United States, it is tempting to conclude that rivers flow north to south. The biggest U.S. rivers—the Mississippi, the Missouri, and the Ohio—all begin in the north and join together to empty into the Gulf of Mexico in the south. However, if you look closely, you will see other rivers flowing in many directions. The main rivers of North America flow north to south, but it appears that it wasn't always that way.

Geologists have long wondered where the thick sandstone rock in Utah came from. Some of the sandstone layers are more than 2,500 feet (750 m) thick. The grains of sand that make up the sandstone had to come from eroded rock—but where? Recent measurements of the ages of some of the sand grains in the rock provide an important clue. The grains are the same age as the Appalachian Mountains near the East Coast. The Appalachians were the only mountain chain on the continent that could have provided the sand grains. But how did the grains end up in the West? The geologists believe that a river as big as the Amazon in South America probably once carried huge amounts of sand as it flowed from the east to some place northwest of Utah. There, the sand was dropped. Later, wind blew the sand to Utah to form thick layers of sandstone.

The river flows across the delta, pushing the sediment farther and farther into the ocean. Gradually, the delta grows outward into the ocean. The upstream end of the delta eventually thickens enough for people to start farming and to build homes and cities.

RIVERS OF ICE

In many mountainous areas, especially far north of the equator and far south, the average temperature is low enough that it snows almost year-round. Snow piles up year after year, and very little of it melts. Eventually, the weight of the pile causes snow at the bottom to turn to ice. When a thick enough layer of ice forms, its weight will start it flowing down valleys or across level plains. A glacier, or river of ice, is formed, and like a liquid river of water, the glacier erodes the rock it passes over. Boulders and pebbles are plucked off the surface of the rock, and they grind on the rock surface. Glaciers flow very slowly, usually only a few yards (meters) per day, but they exert tremendous grinding force. In mountainous areas, this grinding produces steep-walled, U-shaped valleys. Over continents and large islands, the glaciers spread out in all directions like pancake batter poured in a skillet. Greenland and Antarctica have glaciers like this. Thousands of years ago, Earth's climate was much cooler than it is in modern times, and large glaciers covered Canada, the northern half of the United States, and

 Taylor Glacier is a valley glacier in Antarctica. As the glacier melts, it will leave behind humps of hard bedrock, rounded hills, and narrow ridges of rock debris.

Europe. These continental-sized glaciers scraped away soil and piled it in long ridges along the front edges of the ice where it stopped. They left raindrop-shaped rocky mounds and buried tens of thousands of blocks of ice that later melted to form depressions that became small lakes.

Eventually, glaciers reach a dry valley or the ocean. The ice on the front end starts breaking off. Rock is dropped and piled up. The sediment piles up, and erosion of the land is so distinctive that geologists have identified many places where glaciers once flowed but have long since melted away. A great place to see old glaciation is Yosemite National Park in California. The park once had many glaciers flowing together out of different connecting mountain valleys. The erosion caused by the largest glaciers actually scooped away the lower ends of some of the smaller valleys, leaving very steep high cliffs. Streams flowing down these cutoff valleys pour off the cliffs in beautiful waterfalls, dropping hundreds or thousands of feet to the main valleys below.

POUNDING SURF

Another of the ways water erodes the solid Earth to make sediment is through wave action. All the coastal areas of the world are subject to waves that pound the shorelines. The energy in the waves smashes the rocks and pushes the pebbles and sand produced forward and back with each wave. Big rocky cliffs are formed in this way, and sometimes the waves even carve shallow caves in the cliffs where the rock is softer. In places where the wave action is less strong, sandy beaches are created from the rock that has been crushed into its mineral grains. The wave action will create currents that move the sand along the shoreline. When a big storm hits, like a hurricane, the wave action becomes much stronger and entire beaches

Waves crashing against the shore pound away at the rock over the centuries. The pounding often forms odd and beautiful shapes such as these along the Pacific coast at Cape Kiwanda State Natural Area in Oregon.

can be washed out to deeper water. In time, the more gentle waves will repair the damage by moving sand back to the shore.

Where do the waves come from? Most waves are created by wind blowing over the surface of water. You can see this for yourself if you fill a shallow dinner plate with water and gently blow across its surface. Small ripples will form. The ripples forming on the surface of the ocean grow rapidly because they can catch more wind. Soon they become waves that can travel from one side of an ocean to another. The water in the wave does not actually cross the ocean. Instead, the water goes up and down as the wave passes. Waves really transfer the wind energy. The best way to see this is with a Slinky. Have a friend hold one end and you the other. Stretch it out. Shake one end. You will see waves travel through the Slinky to the other end. The material of the Slinky only goes up and down. It is the energy that is transferred by the Slinky.

Waves can grow to be very large when they approach shallow water. The friction with the bottom causes the waves to roll over on themselves and crash on the shore. The crashing can break shoreline rocks and wear away the edges of continents. When giant storms such as hurricanes strike shorelines, heavy wave action can persist for hours or days. The damage to beaches, sand dunes, forests, and homes can be extensive.

Some of the most powerful waves are created when an earthquake occurs. These waves are given the Japanese name *tsunami*. The force of the earthquake propels the waves at high speed across oceans where they crash on opposite shores. Tsunamis can be so powerful that they can wipe away shoreline towns and villages. On December 26, 2004, a massive earthquake under the Indian Ocean triggered a tsunami that struck eleven countries, killing 180,000 people in southeastern Asia.

WIND WEARING

Wind is air in motion. Uneven heating of Earth's surface causes some places to get hotter than others. Earth's dayside is hot and its nightside is cool. Hot air rises and cool air falls. This creates wind.

As an erosion agent, wind might seem like a minor player. After all, wind is just air. What could it accomplish? It accomplishes a great deal. The power in wind increases rapidly with its speed. We have already learned that wind can create destructive ocean waves. It can also create powerful dust storms across arid lands. The air becomes so full of dust and sand that peoplep can't see. The blowing particles will sculpt rock. The erosion is less than that caused by running water, but in time, wind can wear away large masses of rocks. In Utah there is a national park where wind has sculpted beautiful rock arches. Wind can also propel broad

Arches National Park in Utah has more than fifteen hundred rock arches. They have been formed by the faster erosion of soft rock than of surrounding harder rock. The erosion is mainly due to the abrasive effects of windblown sand.

rivers of sand in deserts such as the Sahara in Africa. The sand forms giant sand dunes, or hills, that shift and change as the surface sand is blown. Wind moves the sand from one side of the dune and drops it onto the other. In this way, the dune is gradually picked up and moved by the wind.

CHEMICAL ACTION

Some rocks erode because they dissolve when exposed to the right chemicals. Water is a mild acid, and it can dissolve limestone. Limestone is a sedimentary rock made of the mineral calcite. Rainwater works its way into the limestone cracks and layers and dissolves the rock. Given lots of time, holes in the rock form that link together into a maze of passageways called caves. If the water seeps away from the passageways, dry caves are left behind. New water slowly seeps into the openings and clings to the ceiling of the cave. There it starts to evaporate, and some of the calcite it contains will be deposited. More drops bring more calcite, and the stalactite grows like an icicle, only it takes hundreds of thousands of years to form. Drops that fall to the cave floor deposit their calcite there. Fat and blunt stalagmites grow upward from the floor.

UP OR DOWN

It is easy to tell stalactites from stalagmites in a cave. The trick is knowing where and how they form. The slender stalactites form from drops that cling to the cave ceiling and grow downward. The fat and blunt stalagmites build upward from the cave floor from drops that have splashed there. There are two memory tricks for telling them apart. Stala*ctites* cling tight to the ceiling. Stala*gmites* might reach the ceiling. Stalactites have a letter *C* in their name. *C* is for ceiling. Stalagmites have a *G* in their name. *G* is for ground. Given enough time, stalactites and stalagmites will grow into each other to form columns. The top of the column will be narrow, and the bottom will be broad.

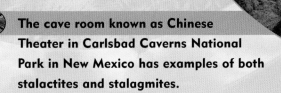

The cave room known as Chinese Theater in Carlsbad Caverns National Park in New Mexico has examples of both stalactites and stalagmites.

CHANGE AND BALANCE

The constructive and destructive forces at work to shape Earth's surface are highly complex. Although things usually happen very slowly, change is constant. Given enough time, mountains rise and fall and entire continents move. Changes in Earth's lithosphere are driven by motions in Earth's mantle, by weather, by gravity, and by living things. It is hard to keep these changes straight, but it helps to follow the journey through time taken by a single mineral grain.

Billions of years ago and deep in Earth's mantle, molten rock is moving upward. Its progress is slow, only a few inches (centimeters) per year. As molten rock melts its way upward, it begins cooling. Very slowly, mineral crystals form. One crystal, in particular, is the mineral quartz, made up of one atom of silicon for every two of oxygen. It is a glassy, tough mineral. The rock it becomes encased in is granite.

Several miles (kilometers) above the quartz grain is Earth's surface. Great forces are pressing on the surface from the east, as the entire continent mass is moving westward at about the same rate at which your fingernails grow. The forces bend and upthrust rock to form a mountain chain. The quartz grain and its surrounding granite move upward to become the core of a mountain. Hundreds of millions of years have passed.

As the mountains thrust upward, weathering and erosion begin attacking them. Daily and seasonal temperature changes cause the rock to expand and contract. Rainwater falls and starts wearing the surface as it washes downward. Chemicals in the water attack the grains. Plants' roots search for cracks to grow in. Water freezes in the cracks and expands. Pieces of the rocks break off. Gravity and running water carry them away. Through eons of time, layer after layer of rock is stripped away. Finally, the granite holding our quartz grain is exposed to the elements. Chemical action softens some of the weaker mineral grains surrounding the quartz and it loosens. The quartz grain begins a journey from the mountaintop to the ocean bottom.

There are many stopping-off places. The mountain stream pours into a wide plain. The grain of sand, along with hundreds of billions of others like it, is dropped at the valley's mouth. A wide fan-shaped deposit builds up. The deposit looks like a delta, but it is on dry land. The quartz grain rests there for tens of thousands of years before a wetter climate increases the water flow. The fan deposit is eroded, and the quartz grain is picked up again. Farther down the valley, the water slows and the quartz grain's progress is greatly slowed. The quartz grain is dropped into a shallow lake, where it becomes part of a sandy beach.

Tens of thousands of years later, the lake is completely filled in with sediment. A wetter period begins again, and a new river washes over the old lake bed and carves a valley. The grain is picked up and carried along until it is deposited in the ocean. The grain becomes a part of a beach. Wave action washes the grain onto the shore and back to shallow water repeatedly. Currents running along the shoreline move the grain miles (kilometers) from the river's mouth.

Gradually, the grain gets buried under thick layers of sand. As the layers accumulate, the sand is cemented together and becomes sandstone. The journey of the grain is not over. It could undergo uplifting again and become part of a mountain or a cliff to be eroded later. It could be buried deeper and deeper where pressures and heat change the sandstone into quartzite. It could be caught with the rock being pulled back down to the mantle for melting as tectonic plates slide into one another. No matter what path the quartz grain takes, the elements that make it up will survive and be recombined into new minerals in the continuous recycling process of Earth's lithosphere. The great battle shaping Earth's surface is really Earth's way of rejuvenating itself.

GLOSSARY

asthenosphere: the upper elastic portion of the mantle upon which the crust moves

core: the iron sphere that is found in Earth's center

dune: a mound of windblown sand or dust

erosion: carrying away of weathered rock particles, such as sand and mud

fossil: marks or remains in rock from ancient life

fumarole: a vent from which volcanic gas escapes into the atmosphere

geyser: a hot spring that periodically erupts with steam and hot-water fountains

glaciers: rivers of thick ice propelled down valleys or across continents by the attraction of gravity

igneous rocks: rocks that form when molten magma or lava cools

lava: molten rock on Earth's surface. (The word is also used to describe the rock formed when lava cools.)

lithosphere: Earth's crust and the upper level of the mantle

magma: molten rock beneath Earth's surface

mantle: the thick layer of rock beneath Earth's crust

metamorphic rocks: rocks that form when existing rocks are subjected to intense heat and pressure

mineral: a naturally occurring collection of elements that are arranged in a crystalline structure

oceans: deep basins of water that separate the continents on Earth

plate tectonics: the theory that states Earth's crust is divided into many large plates that move across Earth's mantle

river: water flowing in a valley

rock: a collection of mineral grains that join together to form the hard material that makes up Earth's lithosphere

sedimentary rocks: rocks that form when sediment such as sand is cemented together or when chemicals such as calcium carbonate crystallize out of ocean water

stalactite: an icicle-like rock formation that grows from the ceiling of a cave

stalagmite: a cone-shaped rock formation that grows upward from the floor of a cave

tsunami: an ocean wave triggered by an earthquake

vent: the opening in Earth's surface from which a volcano erupts

volcanic rock: rock formed from molten lava

weathering: the breakdown of rock by chemical or physical forces

BIBLIOGRAPHY

Bobick, James E., and Naomi E. Balaban, eds. *The Handy Science Answer Book.* Compiled by Science and Technology Department of the Carnegie Library of Pittsburgh. Detroit: Visible Ink Press, 2003.

Davidson, Joh P., Walter E. Reed, and Paul M. Davis. *Exploring Earth: An Introduction to Physical Geology.* 2nd ed. Upper Saddle River, NJ: Prentice Hall, 2001.

"Earth from Space." *NASA.* November 16, 2004. http://earth.jsc .nasa.gov/sseop/efs/ (August 14, 2006).

Fitcher, Lynn S. *A Plate Tectonic Primer.* September 5, 2005. http://csmres.jmu.edu/geollab/Fichter/PlateTect/index.html (August 14, 2006).

Hamblin, W. Kenneth, and Eric H. Christiansen. *Earth's Dynamic Systems.* 10th ed. Upper Saddle River, NJ: Prentice-Hall, 2003.

Lambert, David, and the Diagram Group. *The Field Guide to Geology.* Updated ed. New York: Checkmark Books, 1998.

Luhr, J. F. ed. *Earth.* New York: DK Publishing, 2003.

Mathez, Edmund A., ed. *Earth Inside and Out* (American Museum of Natural History Books). New York: New Press, 2001.

Mathez, Edmund A., and James D. Webster. *The Earth Machine: The Science of a Dynamic Planet.* New York: Columbia University Press, 2004.

Smith, Gary, and Aurora Pun. *How Does Earth Work: Physical Geology and the Process of Science.* Upper Saddle River, NJ: Prentice-Hall, 2005.

Tarbuck, Edward J., Frederick K. Lutgens, and Dennis Tasa. *Earth: An Introduction to Physical Geology.* 8th ed. Upper Saddle River, NJ: Prentice Hall, 2004.

"Understanding Plate Motions." *U.S. Geological Survey.* May 5, 1999. http://pubs.usgs.gov/gip/dynamic/understanding.html (August 14, 2006).

FOR FURTHER INFORMATION

Books

Carruthers, Margaret, and Susan Clinton. *Pioneers of Geology: Discovering Earth's Secrets*. Danbury, CT: Franklin Watts, 2001.

Downs, Sandra. *Earth's Fiery Fury*. Minneapolis: Lerner Publications Company, 2000.

Hooper, Meredith, and Lucia deLeiris. *The Island That Moved*. New York: Viking, 2004.

Johnson, Rebecca L. *Plate Tectonics*. Minneapolis: Twenty-First Century Books, 2006.

Patent, Dorothy Hinshaw. *Shaping the Earth*. New York: Clarion Books, 2000.

Redfern, Martin. *The Kingfisher Young People's Book of Planet Earth*. New York: Kingfisher Books, 1999.

Vogt, Gregory L. *Earth's Core and Mantle: Heavy Metal, Moving Rock*. Minneapolis: Twenty-First Century Books, 2007.

Woods, Michael, and Mary B. Woods. *Earthquakes*. Minneapolis: Lerner Publications Company, 2007.

————. *Volcanoes*. Minneapolis: Lerner Publications Company, 2007.

Websites

Barthelmy, David. *Mineralogy Database*. http://webmineral.com/ This technical site on minerals offers lots of good pictures and very detailed information on mineral properties.

NASA Jet Propulsion Laboratory. *Planetary Photojournal*. http://photojournal.jpl.nasa.gov/ This NASA site features many downloadable pictures of Earth and the other planets.

National Park Service, U.S. Department of the Interior. *Experience Your America*. http://www.nps.gov/ Surf this site to tour the many geological wonders found in national parks. Visit the Grand Canyon, Yellowstone, and Hawaii Volcanoes national parks.

North Dakota and Oregon Space Grant Consortia. *Volcano World*. http://volcano.und.nodak.edu/vw.html
This site provides information on current eruptions, volcano history, and education.

United States Geological Survey. *Photo Glossary of Volcano Terms*. September 4, 2000. http://volcanoes.usgs.gov/Products/Pglossary/pglossary.html
Learn about volcanoes by selecting glossary terms and seeing pictures and explanations of what they mean.

United States Geological Survey. *U.S. Geological Survey*. http://www.usgs.gov/
This site contains a wide range of geological and related information and maps, including an atlas of the United States and aerial photographs.

INDEX

anticlines, 51, 52
Appalachian Mountains, 24, 36, 51, 52–53, 61

basalt, 18, 44
bauxite, 15

calcite, 16, 17, 20, 21, 68
Carlsbad Caverns National Park, 69
caves, 64, 68, 69
Colorado River, 7, 8, 25
continental drift, 38
convection current, 39–40
core, Earth's, 10, 38; inner, 10; outer, 10
crust, Earth's, 13, 14, 32, 35, 40, 44, 45; continental, 12–13, 14, 29; oceanic, 12–13, 14, 29, 36, 39, 40

Earth: core of, 10; formation of, 38–39; location of, 9–10; shaping of, 7–9, 11, 18–23, 70, 73;

supercontinent of, 28–31; temperature inside of, 38
earthquakes, 32, 35, 36, 41, 46, 50, 53, 54, 55, 66
erosion, 8, 9, 18, 19, 23, 25, 26, 27, 43, 52, 57, 62–68, 71; caused by chemical action, 68, 71; caused by glaciers, 62–63; caused by running water, 58–60, 67; caused by waves, 64–66, 67; caused by wind, 66–68. *See also* weathering

faults, 53, 55
feldspar, 16, 17, 21
fumaroles, 44, 47

geysers, 44, 46–47; Old Faithful, 46
gneiss, 8, 26
Grand Canyon, 7, 8, 25, 27
granite, 14, 18, 22, 23, 25, 36, 71
Great Global Rift, 31–32, 33, 36, 37, 38, 39, 41

Hawaiian-Emperor Island Chain, 42, 43

Hawaiian Islands, 41–42, 43, 45, 48, 49; Hawaii, 41, 42, 44, 45

Hess, Henry, 31, 32

Himalayas, 8, 35, 52

hot spots, 44, 45, 46, 48; volcanoes on, 48

hot springs, 44, 47

iron, 15

islands, 7, 9, 41–42, 43, 44–45. *See also* Hawaiian Islands

lava, 18–19, 26, 43, 44, 45, 48–49, 50; types of, 49. *See also* magma

limestone, 8, 20, 21, 52, 68

lithosphere, 11, 38, 40, 70, 73; composition of, 12–15; description of, 12–14; diagram of, 13. *See also* crust, Earth's

magma, 18, 22–23, 26, 33, 36, 37, 48. *See also* lava

mantle, 10–11, 13, 23, 34, 36, 37, 38, 39, 40, 44, 45, 70, 72

Mauna Loa, 41, 45, 48, 49

Mid-Atlantic Ridge, 33, 34, 35, 54

minerals, 14–17, 23, 25, 27, 59, 70–71; properties of, 16, 17

mountains, 7, 9, 11, 12, 22, 24, 25, 36; folded, 51–52; formation of, 32, 34–35, 40, 41, 44, 51–53, 56, 70, 71, 72; longest chain of, 31–32, 33, 34

Mount Fuji, 45, 48

Mount Rainier, 45, 48, 50, 52

New Madrid Fault, 53

Nile River Delta, 8

ocean floor, 33, 36; map of, 32; mapping of, 31. *See also* tectonic plates: oceanic plates

plate tectonics, 32, 33–36, 37, 38, 41, 44

quartz, 15, 16, 17, 18, 21, 23, 71–73

Ring of Fire, 37

rock cycle, 22–23, 24–25; diagram of, 25

rocks, 14, 30; age of, 25; formation of, 34, 38, 45; igneous, 18–19, 22, 25, 26, 27, 39; metamorphic, 21–22, 23, 25, 27; sedimentary, 19–21, 22, 23, 24, 25–26, 27, 68; volcanic, 19, 43. *See also* erosion; rock cycle; weathering

San Andreas Fault, 55

sandstone, 8, 23, 26, 61, 72

San Juan River, 60

sediment, 8, 22, 23, 26, 33, 36, 38, 56, 58, 59, 60, 62, 64, 72. *See also* limestone; rocks: sedimentary; sandstone; shale

seismographs, 54

shale, 8, 21, 22

slate, 21, 22

stalactites, 68, 69

stalagmites, 68, 69

synclines, 51, 52

tectonic plates, 23, 32, 33, 34, 36, 37, 55, 72; collision of, 34–36, 37, 40, 45, 51; continental plates, 36, 39, 40, 45; crustal plates, 39, 40, 52; map of, 35, 37; oceanic plates, 34–36, 38, 39, 45

volcanoes, 6, 7, 19, 24, 25, 35, 36, 37, 40, 43, 45; composite, 45, 50; shield, 45, 48

weathering, 57–58, 70, 71. *See also* erosion

Wegener, Alfred, 28, 29, 31, 32

Yellowstone National Park, 44, 46

Yosemite National Park, 64

ABOUT THE AUTHOR

Gregory L. Vogt holds a doctor of education degree in curriculum and instruction from Oklahoma State University. He began his professional career as a science teacher. He later joined NASA's education programs teaching students and teachers about space exploration. He works in outreach programs for the Kennedy Space Center. He also serves as an educational consultant to Delaware North Parks Services of Spaceport and is the principal investigator for an educational grant with the National Space Biomedical Research Institute. Vogt has written more than seventy children's science books.

PHOTO ACKNOWLEDGMENTS

The images in this book are used with the permission of: PhotoDisc Royalty Free by Getty Images, (cracked earth: main and second ring), (lava: center ring), (vegetation: fourth ring), (sky/clouds: fifth ring), all backgrounds, pp. 2–3, 6, 12, 15, 23, 28, 41, 49, 51, 56, 70; MedioImages Royalty Free by Getty Images, (water: third ring), all backgrounds, p. 2; NASA (stars/nebula: sixth ring), (earth), all backgrounds, pp. 2–3, 4, 8, 74, 76, 78, 80; © David Muench/CORBIS, pp. 7, 69; © Laura Westlund/ Independent Picture Service, pp. 10, 13, 27, 32, 35, 36, 37, 40, 42; © SuperStock, Inc./SuperStock, p. 17 (top); © Mark A. Schneider/Visuals Unlimited, p. 17 (second from top); © Albert J. Copley/Visuals Unlimited, p. 17 (second from bottom); © Dane S. Johnson/Visuals Unlimited, p. 17 (bottom); © Kaj R. Svensson/Photo Researchers, Inc., p. 18; © Bernhard Edmaier/Photo Researchers, Inc., pp. 19, 33; © age fotostock/SuperStock, pp. 20, 43; © Marli Miller/Visuals Unlimited, pp. 21, 50, 60; U.S. Geological Survey Photo Library, p. 24; © Bettmann/CORBIS, p. 29; © Mark Garlick/ Photo Researchers, Inc., p. 30; © Richard Cummins/SuperStock, p. 46; © John Warden/SuperStock, p. 47; © NASA/Photo Researchers, Inc., p. 48; © Dick Roberts/Visuals Unlimited, p. 52; © D. Parker/Photo Researchers, Inc., p. 55; © James Steinberg/Photo Researchers, Inc., p. 58; © Ann B. Keiser/SuperStock, p. 63; © Jim Corwin/Photo Researchers, Inc., p. 65; © Visions of America/SuperStock, p. 67. Front Cover: PhotoDisc Royalty Free by Getty Images, (cracked earth: main and second ring), (lava: center ring), (vegetation: fourth ring), (sky/clouds: fifth ring); MedioImages Royalty Free by Getty Images, (water: third ring); NASA, (stars/nebula: sixth ring). Back Cover: PhotoDisc Royalty Free by Getty Images, (cracked earth); NASA, (earth). Spine: PhotoDisc Royalty Free by Getty Images, (cracked earth).